William Buell Sprague, Princeton Theological Seminary

A Discourse Addressed to the Alumni of the Princeton Theological Seminary

April 30, 1862, on occasion of the completion of its first half century

William Buell Sprague, Princeton Theological Seminary

A Discourse Addressed to the Alumni of the Princeton Theological Seminary
April 30, 1862, on occasion of the completion of its first half century

ISBN/EAN: 9783337169541

Printed in Europe, USA, Canada, Australia, Japan

Cover: Foto ©Lupo / pixelio.de

More available books at **www.hansebooks.com**

A

DISCOURSE

ADDRESSED TO

THE ALUMNI

OF THE

𝔓𝔯𝔦𝔫𝔠𝔢𝔱𝔬𝔫 𝔗𝔥𝔢𝔬𝔩𝔬𝔤𝔦𝔠𝔞𝔩 𝔖𝔢𝔪𝔦𝔫𝔞𝔯𝔶,

APRIL 30, 1862,

ON OCCASION OF

THE COMPLETION OF ITS FIRST HALF CENTURY.

BY WILLIAM B. SPRAGUE, D. D.

———◆———

WITH AN APPENDIX,

CONTAINING NOTICES OF THE OTHER COMMEMORATIVE EXERCISES.

———◆———

ALBANY:
STEAM PRESS OF VAN BENTHUYSEN.
1862.

DISCOURSE.

FELLOW ALUMNI AND DEAR BRETHREN:

It would be an offence against the proprieties of the hour, against the instincts of nature, and even the dictates of religion, to suppose that our hearts were not now moved by a common impulse, and our thoughts flowing in the same channel. In coming back to this endeared spot, to keep this commemorative day, we have, I suppose, by common consent, left all matters of private and individual interest behind us. We have come to unite in an offering of reverence, and gratitude, and filial devotion to the mother who has cherished and trained us, and then dismissed us with her blessing, and sent us forth to our work. We have come to offer to God thanksgiving, not only for his manifold tokens of kindness to ourselves, in the various fields we have occupied, but for that unbroken stream of bounty and grace, which, during all these years, He has been pouring upon our beloved Seminary. We have come to look on each other's faces again in the land of the living; to refresh our spirits by the interchange of kind thoughts and grateful remembrances; and though we shall meet the graves of many of our brethren on the field we are to traverse, and cannot but pause in tenderness and sadness by the side of them, yet the transition to the glorious world beyond is too easy to allow them to cast upon us more than a momentary shadow. It is chiefly a work of the heart then, in the form of communion with each other, and, may I not add, with a portion of the General Assembly and Church of the First Born, that we are assembled here to perform.

The occasion, you perceive, gives me no choice of a subject. There are numerous topics, bearing more or less directly on the general subject of Theological Education, from which I might perhaps select, without doing any great violence to the occasion; but I am sure you would regard *any* abstract discussion as but a poor response to the distinctive claims of the day. In your heart, if not with your lips, you would be quoting Solomon against me, where he says, "To every thing there is a season." You would say, Other themes for other places and other times; but here, to-day, the only befitting theme is the PRINCETON

THEOLOGICAL SEMINARY. I do not complain of the restraint which the occasion imposes upon me—I am rather glad to be shut up in so green a pasture.

The thought which I propose now to illustrate, is at once the most general and the most obvious that suggests itself in connection with the occasion—namely, that THIS INSTITUTION IS A MIGHTY POWER—mighty in its ELEMENTS, mighty in its OPERATIONS.

The first element of this power is to be found in *the spirit in which the Institution originated.* The spirit of any age, or of the Church, or any portion of the Church, at any given period, is never a matter of accident, or the product of causes that have had only a brief existence—on the contrary, it has had a long train of antecedents, and is the result of the combined influences of many minds, and perhaps of several generations. The Presbyterian Church in this country, from her beginning, was marked by true Christian nobility: on the very first page of her records are names which will always remain proof against the oblivious influence of time. While she was yet in her minority, unhappily she stood forth before the world as a house divided against itself; but, even then, she had her noble spirits on each side; and, though they were not working *harmoniously*, the Head of the Church was overruling their independent and even conflicting movements for the correction of her errors, and the ultimate increase of her energies. As the re-union marked a bright period in her history, so it proved a starting point for yet more signal triumphs; and though, in common with every other Christian denomination, she had a thorny path to traverse during the War of the Revolution, yet, besides showing herself baptized with the fire of Christian patriotism, she was prosecuting her appropriate mission up to the full measure of her ability. And in the generation that came out of that conflict, as well as in the one that immediately succeeded, our Church had many choice spirits, to whose influence in guiding, controlling, elevating, it were not easy to fix a limit. Here we reach the point where the great idea of establishing a Theological Seminary, to meet the increasing wants of the Church, was first developed. Three generations at least had performed their work and passed away, leaving the results in a widely extended ecclesiastical body, in an elevated tone of public spirit, and in a just appreciation of an enlightened as well as earnest ministry. And now that the fulness of time for this great work had come, not only was the general state of the public mind, in a good degree, prepared for it, but there were men found suitable to conduct the enterprise;—men who united to a sober, comprehensive, far reaching intellect a heart in which the love of Christ and of his Church was the ruling passion. The Presbytery of Philadelphia, of which Doctors GREEN and JANEWAY were prominent members, had the honour of originating the overture to the General Assembly, in which this noble conception was embodied; and it was certainly highly creditable to the catholic spirit of the Assembly of 1809, that the Chairman of the Committee, to whom this important subject was referred, was Dr. DWIGHT, President of Yale College, who was a delegate that year from the General Association of Connecticut. The report of the Committee was marked by great wisdom, and suggested three different ways in which the exigency might be met—namely, the establishment of one Seminary that should be central in the Church; or the establishment of two,—one in the North and one in the South; or the establishment of one within the bounds of each Synod. Agreeably to the suggestion of the

2

Committee, these several plans were referred to the consideration of all the Presbyteries, with a request that they would respectively signify their preference at the next meeting of the Assembly; and, when the returns came to be made in 1810, the question was decided in favour of the one central institution. The next step was the drafting of a Plan of the proposed Seminary; and to this service Doctors GREEN, WOODHULL, ROMEYN, MILLER, ALEXANDER, RICHARDS and ARMSTRONG—all men of note in the Church, and some of them men of extraordinary power—were designated. Of the instrument which they produced, (said to have been from the pen of Dr. Green,) I will only say that it was worthy of the honoured names affixed to it. Thus it appears that, while this Institution had its origin in a watchful regard to the interests of the Church, its foundations were laid by some of the master-builders in Zion; and I am sure you will agree with me in recognizing in this fact one of the leading elements of its power.

I find another in *the felicitous selection of the place where the Institution should be located.* It might seem, at first, that the prevalent idea of the Presbyteries, which was also sanctioned by

the General Assembly, that there should be one
great *central* institution for the accommodation of
the whole Church, was not very rigidly adhered
to, inasmuch as the position actually selected had
a large majority of Presbyteries, as well as a
much more extended territory, South of it. This
arrangement doubtless had its origin in the spirit
of fraternal conciliation, and in the general desire
to accomplish the greatest amount of good. It
was perceived at once that this place offered facili-
ties for the establishment and growth of such a
seminary, that were to be found nowhere else;
and to this weighty consideration our fathers were
willing to sacrifice all personal preferences. Besides, they were well aware that they were making provision for the Church as she then was,
and not as she would be at some distant day; and
doubtless they foresaw what has actually come to
pass,—that, as she extended the bounds of her
habitation, she would plant other similar institutions to meet her increasing necessities. Nor is
it to be supposed that they wholly ignored the
fact that this place is easily accessible from the
New England States; for there was a relationship
existing then between our denomination and the
Congregationalists of New England, that has since

ceased; and, though the Andover Seminary was at that time in successful operation, it was doubtless anticipated—and the event justified the anticipation—that many young men from among our Northern neighbours would prefer an education here to one in their own well-endowed and honoured Institution. These, it may be presumed, were some of the considerations that led the Assembly to that more liberal construction of the expressed will of the Church, that fixed the Seminary so far North of the actual centre of the domain of Presbyterianism.

But what were the particular circumstances which combined to give this place an advantage over any other that could be selected? First of all, it is a *lovely* spot; where nature has been even prodigal of both her bounties and her beauties; where there is a healthful atmosphere to breathe, and rich prospects to gaze upon and admire. So, too, it is a *retired* spot, and therefore favourable to study, to devotion, to the general culture of both the intellect and the heart. It cannot be denied that a Theological Seminary, in the midst of a crowded population, has some advantages peculiar to itself; particularly in the opportunities it affords for active usefulness in ministering to the spiritual

wants of the ignorant and depraved; but is it not
at least questionable whether these advantages
are not more than counterbalanced by the dis-
traction and turmoil, and especially the manifold
temptations to a spirit of worldliness, incident to a
great city ? But this Institution, though exposed to
few disturbing influences, is far from occupying a
too secluded position—here and hereabouts are all
the advantages for social enjoyment and culture
that any student can reasonably desire. And then
it is to be borne in mind that this quiet place is
about equi-distant from the two largest cities on
the Continent ; that as either can now be reached
in a couple of hours, so the advantages of both are
easily accessible ; and that our students can procure books, or any thing else, from either of these
cities just about as readily as if they lived on
Broadway or Chestnut Street. But probably the
controlling circumstance that led to the selection
of this spot, was that here was *already established
a great literary institution*, which had, from its
beginning, been identified with the Presbyterian
Church ; an institution whose history was, to a
great extent, the history of illustrious names ; and
whose fame and influence had already penetrated to
the extremities of the land. When the Seminary

was born, the College threw a protecting arm
around her, as if she had been an adopted child.
The College Library was our library. Our recitation room was in one of the College buildings.
Our place of worship was the College Hall. One-
third of the preaching we listened to on Sabbath
morning was from the venerable President of the
College. Our evening discussions were often en-
livened by the wit and genius of one of the College Professors,—I mean the lamented LINDSLY.
In short, it is not too much to say that the benign
influence of the College was all-pervading. As
the Seminary grew in years, she grew also in
strength, and, after a while, she went up and took
possession of her own noble home; and, in pro-
cess of time, she became independent in respect
to all her accommodations. But she has never
cut loose from the College in any such sense as to
forget her early debt of gratitude, or to decline or
undervalue the benefits of an enduring intimacy.
The Professors in the Seminary and the Officers
of the College have always been fellow-helpers in
every good work; and I venture to say that there
are few who cherish a more grateful remembrance
of CARNAHAN, and DOD, and HOPE, than our sur-
viving Professors who were associated with them.

The truth is that the two institutions have, in various ways, ministered to the advantage of each other; and each of them holds a higher place to-day,—the one in the world of Letters, the other in the domain of Theology,—than if they had not been walking together for half a century in one another's light.

There is yet another circumstance, worthy of being noticed, that designates this place as peculiarly fitted to be the seat of a Theological Seminary—I refer to the fact that it is *the depository of so much venerable dust.* Our fathers, in fixing upon this spot, did not forget that the graves of BURR, and EDWARDS, and DAVIES, and WITHERSPOON were here; and that the illustrious SAMUEL STANHOPE SMITH was lingering in the twilight of life, just ready to be gathered; and, if they could have thrown themselves forward, fifty years, they would have found that family of honoured graves more than doubled. Those graves are the silent representatives of some of the brightest spirits which have emigrated from earth to Heaven; and, to every minister of the Gospel, and every candidate for the ministry, they speak most impressively of being faithful unto the death, and of the crown and the throne, with which fidelity shall be rewarded. Is it not a privilege to be living within a few moments' walk of a group of monuments, that have names inscribed upon them, which are as household words all over Evangelical Christendom? Is it not reasonable to believe that many a young man who comes hither to be trained for his sacred work, while he sits with docility and delight at the feet of the living teacher, sometimes gets a fresh baptism of spiritual influence by waiting at the graves of the glorified dead? Is it too much to suppose that the very atmosphere of this Institution has been rendered more pure from its connection with the memories of these departed sages and saints?

Enough, I trust, has been said to show that the power of this Seminary is derived partly from its favourable position. A yet more important element of this power is *the character of the minds that have controlled it.*

The conception, the beginning, even the establishment, of a great institution is nothing more than the opening of a field for gifted and well trained minds to labour in; and unless the services of such minds can be put in requisition, the design of the institution can never be accomplished. Great moral enterprises do not work out their

legitimate results by mere mechanical force : even
the Almighty Architect of the Universe, though
He has been pleased to subject the Kingdoms of
both Nature and Providence to fixed laws, yet
never, for a moment, withdraws his eye from the
minutest of his works, or leaves a single event to
occur without his guiding and controlling agency
—surely then it were preposterous to imagine that
human wisdom should breathe into any of its
plans or its works a principle of life, which, if not
absolutely self-sustaining, would require but little
care or effort for its preservation.   After this
Seminary had been created, by an Act of the General Assembly, and the whole Church had pronounced the work very good, the enterprise might
have been rendered utterly abortive by being
confided to an inadequate supervision and direction.   But, instead of that, the same noble spirits
that had projected and founded it, became its
Guardians and Professors; and, as they passed
away, others, upon whom their mantles fell, entered into their labours; and thus the Seminary
. has passed the perils of youth, and reached a vigorous and prosperous manhood.   Never could this
point have been attained but for the large measure of intellectual foresight, and comprehensive-
3

ness, and accomplishment, of love to the Church, of reliance on the wisdom, and power, and grace from above, and of harmony of counsel and effort, which have characterized those to whom the destinies of the Institution have thus far been committed.

If we glance at the list of the *Directors* of the Seminary, the first name on which our eye rests, is that of the venerable ASHBEL GREEN,—whose majestic bearing seemed to say that he was born to rule; and who, during many of his later years, stood as an almost solitary representative of the ministry of a preceding generation. His commanding presence fitly represented his force of intellect and force of will. He was sternly unyielding in his regard to what he believed right, and in his opposition to what he considered wrong; and some of his demonstrations might have indicated, especially to those who saw him only at a distance, that there was an excess of iron in his moral constitution; but those who were privileged to get nearer to his heart, and to witness the air of graceful kindness which he diffused around his own fireside; who knew the comforting words that he uttered to the sorrowful, and the encouraging words that he addressed to the

desponding, and the large charities that he dis-
pensed to the poor, needed no other evidence that
there was strung in his bosom a chord, not only
of high generosity but of tender sympathy. Besides serving the College in this place, in the relations of both Professor and President,—the latter
for a long course of years, he exercised his ministry, for a quarter of a century, in connection with
one of the most influential churches on the Continent, and at a period which identified him with
some of the leading events of both our civil and
ecclesiastical history. He shone, perhaps, nowhere
more brightly than in the pulpit. His discourses
were simple and natural in their construction;
of a deeply evangelical and practical tone; full of
appropriate and luminous thought; and delivered
with an air of dignity and impressiveness that
scarcely left it at any one's option whether or not
to be an attentive hearer. The clouds of old age
had settled around him some time before his de-
parture; but I believe they were at no time so
dark and heavy but the beams of the Sun of Right-
eousness passed through them into his soul. It was
an auspicious omen to the Seminary that such a
veteran in wisdom and piety should have had such
a place assigned to him, and especially that he

should have occupied the chair of the President of the Board of Directors for so long a period.

The name of Dr. Green, at the head of the list of Directors, is followed by more than a hundred other names, some of which are associated with princely liberality and public spirit, others with the highest order of pulpit eloquence, or executive power, or both combined, while most of them have commanded, in a high degree, the respect and confidence of the Church. In looking over this honoured list, I find not a few, who, for their exalted character as well as faithful services, are well worthy of grateful commemoration; and, but for the invidiousness of making a selection, and the fear of exhausting your patience, I would gladly pay a passing tribute to a goodly number of them. Indeed, there are two bright names on this catalogue, which have so lately become associated with the grave, and which, withal, suggest such precious memories, that I am sure you would not be willing that I should pass them without at least a kindly commemorative word. Need I say that I refer to Van Rensselaer and Murray.

Cortlandt Van Rensselaer had his birth and education amidst decidedly Christian influences, and yet amidst those temptations to a life of indolent ease, which are always incident, especially in this country, to a condition of great opulence and worldly consideration. Happily, in his case, Christianity early assumed the dominion in his heart, so that he passed safely the ordeal to which Providence subjected him, and came out of the walks of the most elegant refinement into one of the humblest of all the fields of ministerial labour. And that mission of good-will to the poor slaves he would gladly have continued, but for the appearance of certain clouds in the distant horizon, that have since covered the whole heavens, and are now discharging their contents in a tempest of fire. We find him next engaged in planting a Presbyterian Church in a beautiful village in this neighbourhood, where none had before existed; and, after a few years of self-denying and eminently useful labour there, he took the responsible position of Secretary of the General Assembly's Board of Education, which he held until the disease of which he died had well-nigh run its course. As he was not only a Director, but an alumnus, of the Seminary, so he was always devoted to its interests; and the office which he held during the greater part of his professional life,—discharging its duties not only most faithfully but gratuitously,

placed him at the head of one of the great foun-
tains of influence by which the Seminary is sustained. Who that knew him will ever forget the
fertility of his mind in projects of Christian usefulness, and the exuberance of his charity in carry-
ing them into effect? Who can forget the kindli-
ness of his smile; the meekness and modesty of his
spirit; the firmness with which he adhered to his
own mature convictions, and the graceful facility
and generous indulgence with which he met the
adverse opinions of others; his practical oblivious-
ness of worldly rank; his wit, sometimes taking
the form of a delicate innuendo, and sometimes
doing the work of a two-edged sword; his zeal
and energy, shrinking from no sacrifices, halting
at no obstacles, and revealing a heart deeply in
communion with Him, who, though He was rich,
for our sakes became poor? His death was the
signal for mourning much beyond the limits of his
own communion. The marble that marks the place
of his grave, might well bear the inscription,—
"An exalted specimen of sanctified humanity."

But scarcely had the mind of the Church been
withdrawn from the heavy calamity sustained in
his death, before the tidings were flying over the
land that NICHOLAS MURRAY, a kindred spirit, had,

by a single step, passed from the fulness of health
and usefulness to his reward. Murray was born
with extraordinary qualities of both mind and
heart; but he was born, and had his early training,
amidst the cold shadows of Romanism. By a
train of circumstances which were little of his own
devising, he was separated from his earliest religious
associations, and was brought across the
ocean, first to cast away his inherited errors, and
then to be baptized with the Holy Ghost. In due
time, he went forth from this School of the Prophets,
and, like the great Apostle, whose spirit he
so largely shared, became an earnest and powerful
defender of the faith which he had seemed born
to oppose. For upwards of thirty years, and until
his Master called him home, he was always in the
high places of Zion, and always had his armour
on, ready to obey any summons. He had strongly
marked national characteristics, but they were so
many irresistible attractions. His face reflected
not only his clear and comprehensive intellect,
but his genial, loving and sympathetic spirit. No
child of sorrow, no victim of temptation, no subject
of poverty, could ever be brought to his notice,
but his heart, his lips, his hand, involuntarily
opened to administer the needed consolation, coun-

sel, or relief. In the pulpit he spake words of wisdom and of weight, and with an air of authority that continually pointed upward to his Divine commission. In the deliberative assembly his presence was always recognized as a power. Through the press his intellect delivered itself of much profound practical wisdom, and the elements of conviction were lodged even in the coruscations of his wit. When his work was done, his hands were still nerved to do more. The Church gazed wishfully after him, and felt that one of her strong rods was broken.

In connection with the Board of Directors, I may mention the Board of *Trustees* also,—on whom devolves the chief management of the financial interests of the Seminary. And here we find another noble body of men,—some of whom have been conspicuous in the different professions, some in the field of judicial honour, some in the circles of commercial enterprise, some in the walks of general philanthropy, while all have been skilfully, watchfully, earnestly engaged in placing the institution on higher and firmer ground, by the successful disposition and gradual enlargement of its pecuniary resources. At the head of this list, and as a fitting representation of

it, stand the justly cherished names of ANDREW
KIRKPATRICK and SAMUEL BAYARD,—both synonymes
for wisdom and purity, benevolence and honour.

Such, then, are the minds by which this Institution, in respect to its outward and more general
concerns, has been controlled; and, surely, under
a conduct so wise and energetic, it were reasonable to suppose that, by this time, it should have
reached a vigorous maturity. But it is the character, not of its Directors and Trustees merely,
but especially of its *Professors*, to which we are to
look for the secret of its rapid and healthful
development. I cannot speak of them all in
detail, as my feelings would incline me, because—
thanks to a Gracious Providence—a portion of them
are yet alive to hear the testimony I should render; but I may say of them, in general, that,
though they have exhibited a diversity of gifts,
yet all have had the same spirit;—a spirit of
singular devotedness to the interests of the Institution—all have been men who have well established their claim upon the gratitude of the Church,
and whose memory the Church will treasure, as a
sacred deposit, in her own bosom. The day will
come—though I would fain hope it may be distant—when the characters of those who now
4

occupy these chairs of honourable usefulness, will become legitimate subjects for delineation; and I have no fear that those on whom the office shall devolve, will find it other than a grateful and easy one; but, meanwhile, we may be allowed to linger for a little among the graves of the departed, and refresh both our memories and our hearts by calling up some of their admirable characteristics.

First on the starred list appears the venerable name of ARCHIBALD ALEXANDER ;—a circumstance that reflects double honour upon the Church at that period ; for it was alike creditable to her that she had such a man within her limits, and that she had the wisdom to place him where his influence would operate with the greatest power. He came hither with the benefit of a large experience, both academic and pastoral ; and the event more than justified the high expectations which had been founded upon his reputation, both in Virginia and in Philadelphia. The feature of his character, which was perhaps more obvious and all-pervading than any other, was a well-nigh matchless simplicity. You saw this, first, in all that pertained to his exterior—the movements of his body, the utterances of his lips, the very expression of his countenance, you felt were in perfect harmony

with the laws of his own individual constitution.
And the same characteristic impressed itself upon
the workings of his mind. Though the best productions of many of the best writers, in every
part and every period of the Church, lay in his
memory as so much well arranged material, and
though he knew how to appropriate it to the best
advantage, and it had even become essentially
incorporated with his own thoughts, yet it never
interfered in the least with the perfect individu-
ality of his intellectual operations. Whatever he
produced, whether orally or with his pen, had his
own image and superscription so deeply wrought
into it that its genuineness could hardly become
a matter of question. And his simplicity was
perfected in the movements of his moral nature—
and here it discovered itself in a frankness that
never dissembled; in an independence that never
faltered; in an integrity that would have maintained itself even in the face of martyr fires. In
all the appropriate duties of his Professorship, he
was alike able and faithful. Not only his lectures,
but his less formal communications to the students,—his criticisms upon their performances,
his solution of their difficulties, and, above all, those
never to be forgotten Sunday afternoon talks on

practical and experimental religion, all showed a richness and promptness of thought, and a depth of piety, which, I am sure, none of us can recall without admiration. What he was as a Preacher you who have heard him can never forget; and you who have not heard him can never know. I will only say that here, as every-where else, he was the very personification of naturalness; and when his inventive and richly stored mind was set vigorously to work in the pulpit, under the combined action of physical health and strong moral forces, he sometimes held his audience by a power absolutely irresistible. The great and good Dr. John H. Rice told me that he once heard him preach to a few people assembled in a private dwelling in Virginia, when he became perfectly transfigured, and his audience as perfectly electrified; and he did not hesitate to pronounce it the highest effort of pulpit eloquence to which he had ever listened. In his descent to the grave, there was a beautiful demonstration of his humility, his faith, his love to God and man,—of all those qualities which had constituted the strength of his character and the glory of his life.

Dr. Alexander was sole Professor but a single year. In 1813, the revered and beloved name of

SAMUEL MILLER became associated with his; and
the relation, thus established, continued a source
of mutual blessing, and a field for cordial co-
operation, for nearly forty years. I will venture
to speak of some of the different phases of Dr.
Miller's character somewhat in the order in which
they presented themselves to me. In the summer
of 1813, and a few weeks only before he entered
on his Professorship, I passed a Sabbath in New
York, and the excellent report of him which I
had often heard in New England, took me to the
then new church in Wall street, one part of the
day. I saw before me in the pulpit a man of a
perfectly symmetrical form, of a countenance expressive at once of mildness, dignity and intelli-
gence, and altogether, as it seemed to me, of rare
personal attractions. Though his voice was not
powerful, or susceptible of any great variety of
inflection, his utterance was perfectly distinct, and
his whole manner evinced thoughtfulness and culture. His discourse (I speak of it with the more
confidence, for I heard it again after I became a
student here) was distinguished for lucid arrangement, for impressive scriptural thought, for great
propriety and elegance of diction, for being thoroughly exhaustive of its subject, and in some parts

for the very sublimity of pathos. It is due to candour to say that I always regarded this as one of his most felicitous efforts; and yet, in its general character, it was but a fair specimen of his preaching. The next time I saw him was three years later, in his own study, when I presented to him a letter designed to procure my introduction to the Seminary. His kindly and almost paternal spirit, breathing through his polished and dignified manner, awakened in me a feeling at once of reverence and affection; and this mingled feeling never forsook me in all my subsequent intercourse with him; and it is the offering which I love to make to his memory to this day. Those fine qualities of mind and heart which were so beautifully reflected in his manners, constituting him the highest type of a Christian gentleman, rendered his presence any-where a benediction. There was a singular grace and fitness in all his words and actions. He had much of the spirit of generous conciliation and forbearance, but it was qualified by an unwavering fidelity to his own well considered and conscientious judgments. His character, as it came out in his daily life, was, to his students, one unbroken lesson of love and wisdom. And his meetings with us in the reci-

tation room were as creditable to his intellect as
to his heart : for, while the influence of his bland
and considerate manner, there as every-where,
operated as a charm, we always had presented
to us a luminous, well digested and highly satis-
factory view of the subject which engaged our
attention. Dr. Miller lived to feel the infirmities
of age, but not to be the subject of a paralyzed
intellect, or to witness any waning of the interest
of the Church in respect to him. I was one of
those who were privileged to see him, when he
was standing almost in the presence of death. I
never heard such sublime words, expressive at
once of trust and victory, as then fell from his
lips. The chariot was already there ; and it was
but a few days after that I heard he had ascended.

There is yet another Professor, who has died
while in connection with the Seminary, and so
recently that the numerous tributes which his
death called forth are still fresh in the memories
of all of us—I refer, as you know, to the gifted
and accomplished ADDISON ALEXANDER. I suppose
I may say, without the fear of contradiction, that
a nobler specimen of the Divine workmanship has
rarely appeared, in the form of a human mind,
than he exhibited. To have possessed any one

faculty in the measure in which he possessed all, would have been enough to constitute a man of mark. His facility at acquiring knowledge of every kind, and especially language, was perhaps without a known parallel; and this, in connection with an untiring industry, gives us the clew to his vast acquisitions. His genius was alike brilliant and powerful—it was equally at home in the heights and in the depths—it could breathe in the zephyr; it could flash in the lightning; it could ride in the storm. The effect of his preaching is thought to have been lessened by the rapidity of his utterance; but his published discourses are a model in respect to both beauty and strength. As a teacher, he not only communicated from stores that seemed inexhaustible, and with a fluency that never hesitated, and a perspicuity that forbade misapprehension, but, by an almost magical influence, he quickened the minds of his pupils into a fervid enthusiasm, which was at once a stimulus to their faculties, and a pledge of their success. He was shy and distant in common intercourse; but those who knew him well, testify that he had not only a large and generous heart, but a strong susceptibility to social enjoyment. For more than twenty years, he shone here, a star of the first magnitude; and the day that saw that star sink beneath the horizon, was a day of deep and widespread mourning.

There have been two other Professors in the Seminary, who have finished their earthly course, though neither of them died until some time after his connection with the Seminary ceased—I refer to JOHN BRECKENRIDGE and JAMES W. ALEXANDER. Both of them performed good service here; but, as each resigned his Professorship after two years, we must doubtless look elsewhere for the monuments of their highest usefulness. Dr. BRECKENRIDGE was a man of brilliant and attractive qualities, of commanding presence, of an earnest, heroic and generous spirit, and of great control of the popular mind. For several years he held the pastoral office in a large city, discharging its duties with great acceptance and success; but perhaps the years in which he accomplished most for the Church, were those in which he was employed in aid of two of our most prominent objects of Christian benevolence. Some of his discourses, and especially of his anniversary speeches, in behalf of these objects, have rarely been exceeded as specimens of manly and effective eloquence.

5

Dr. ALEXANDER inherited many of the fine qualities, not only of his father, but, it is believed, of his maternal grandfather also,—the far-famed Dr. JAMES WADDEL. Like his father, he was a model of simplicity in every thing; while he had probably more of graceful culture than his father could claim. He had a mind of great richness, great delicacy, and exquisite susceptibility to every form of beauty. His thoughts always seemed fresh and glowing. His pen rarely moved but it flew; and yet in the record which it made, we sometimes recognize the ingenious speculations of the philosopher, and sometimes the gorgeous creations of the poet. He was distinguished for habits of sanctity and devotion; but there was born with him, and there always remained with him, a vein of playful humour, that he knew better how to control than others knew how to resist. His preaching was at once attractive and instructive. Multitudes thronged to hear him, and not a few met in his ministrations the converting and sanctifying power of God. Both these eminent ministers, though the period of their actual connection with the Seminary was brief, were yet always on the alert to promote its interests, and carried a strong affection for it to their graves.

Estimate now the evidence which has been presented that the character of the Professors of this
Seminary forms a mighty element of power. Can
any one believe that men of so much intellectual
and moral force can have been here,—some of
them for so long a period,—in the vigorous and
diligent use of their faculties, without making
this Institution one of the strongholds of Zion?
Especially can any one believe this, when the
influence of the Directors and Trustees is taken
in connection with that of the Professors, thus
securing the wisest management, as well as the
most faithful guidance and the ablest instruction?

Yet another element of strength in this Institution is *the bounty by which it has been sustained.*
We all know that such an institution as this could
never be established and maintained but at a vast
expense. Here is a capacious and commodious
building devoted to the use of the students. Here
are dwellings for the occupancy of the Professors.
Here is a fine, tasteful edifice for the accommodation of the Library; to say nothing of the choice and
extensive Library which it accommodates. Then
again, here are five well endowed Professorships;
and probably about thirty Scholarships, (though
the number is nominally considerably greater,)

which meet, in a great measure, the exigencies of
an equal number of indigent students. Surely,
all this could never have been done, if the bounty
of the Church had not flowed hither as a river.
The Seminary has had, still has, individual benefactors, whose donations are not only honourable
but princely; and though delicacy forbids me here
to pronounce their names, gratitude has already
inscribed them on an imperishable record. And
I cannot forbear to refer to the fact, the announcement of which, a few moments since, has filled us
with admiration and gratitude, that two of these
benefactors have impressed their own bright mark
upon this day, by making it the occasion of an
offering that is itself grand enough to form an
epoch in the history of the Institution.* And the
Church, as a body, or at least no inconsiderable
portion of it, has, with a willing mind, sent hither
large offerings, sanctified by faith and prayer.

---

* It may not be improper here to state that the donation referred to
was fifty thousand dollars, from Messrs. ROBERT L. and ALEXANDER
STUART, to be applied, in several different ways, for the benefit of the
Seminary. Another donation, of thirty-five thousand dollars, has been
recently made by Mr. JOHN C. GREEN, for the endowment of a new
Professorship. Each of these gentlemen had so signalized himself by
his previous benefactions to the Seminary, that these generous and
graceful gifts were less a matter of surprise than of thankfulness and
rejoicing. It is well known that the beautiful building, containing the
Library, is but a magnificent item in the sum of the contributions of
Mr. JAMES LENOX.

Is it too much, then, to say that the mighty power in whose presence we stand, has its being, at least in a subordinate sense, in the spirit of Christian Charity?

The last element of this power which I will ask you to consider, is *the influence of the great numbers who have been educated here, reacting upon the Institution itself.* I do not say that every individual who has had his training on this ground, has gone away satisfied; for I well know that there are some, who, if there was nothing on earth to find fault with, would vent their spleen against the sun, moon and stars: but I do say with confidence that our students have, with very few exceptions, carried away with them a grateful sense of the benefits received here, which has manifested itself, as opportunity has presented, in substantial acts of good-will. You do not expect a child, of even ordinary sensibility, to forget his early home,—no matter how great may be the distance that separates him from it. You do not expect even the alien, if he has the heart of a man, to ignore the hand that has been stretched out for his guidance, or opened for his relief, as soon as he has passed the range of its movements—and not more reasonable were it to expect that those who have been theologically nurtured here, should forget the helping, forming influence, as soon as they have passed from under it. I tell you, again, they do not forget it—and, more than that, it weighs upon them as an ever present, cherished obligation, keeping their hearts strong, and their hands nerved, for any good service it may be in their power to render. Indeed, they are always serving the Seminary just in proportion to the measure of their fidelity and usefulness in the Church; for they are its epistle, known and read of all men. Wherever you meet one of its alumni, you have a right to assume, until it is proved to the contrary, that you have found one who always bears it on his heart, and is ready, according to his ability, to lend a helping hand for the promotion of its interests. Well may an Institution, with such an army of auxiliaries scattered all over the land, repose securely in a sense of its own stability.

I have endeavoured to show that this Seminary is a power mighty in its elements—let us see now whether it is not equally mighty in its OPERATIONS.

I say, then, the influence which this Institution has exerted, still exerts, is *diversified, and yet harmonious.* Its records show that there is scarcely a

department of ministerial or Christian usefulness
in which it has not been largely and most credit-
ably represented. Of course its grand object is
to make able and faithful ministers of the Gospel ;
and the great business of the ministry is to fulfil
the Divine ordinance in the preaching of the
Gospel. Nevertheless, the sacred office, in respect
to its particular duties, is somewhat modified by a
variety of circumstances ; and, in some instances,
it becomes incorporated with other kindred voca-
tions. While the individuals concerned appear
occasionally, perhaps frequently, in the pulpit,
they are entrusted with the supervision and direction of the different branches of the machinery
by which the Church is doing her great work ;
and it may be that, while the literal preacher
may seem to be almost lost,—perhaps in the quiet
round of a teacher's duties, perhaps in the conduct of some grand evangelical enterprise, he may
really be accomplishing more for the Church than
if he could multiply himself into half a dozen
stated preachers. I know not whether the office
of a Christian minister ever combines more of
privation and self-sacrifice with more of efficiency
and glory, than when held by the faithful Foreign
Missionary ;—the man who goes forth, in the

strength of God's grace, to battle with the prince of darkness in the very heart of his earthly dominion. It devolves upon him to strike the first blow for the deliverance perhaps of a vast empire from the deepest intellectual and moral degradation ; to supply the first material for the mind to act upon, as it is waking out of the slumber of ages; to commence the re-construction of the whole fabric of society, by substituting a Christian for a Heathen basis—but no less than one hundred and twenty-seven of our students have become Foreign Missionaries; besides seven more who have already been designated to the same office— that is, they have gone, or are going, to carry the Gospel either to the savages on our borders, or the far off Pagans,—both sitting alike within the shadow of death. No man occupies a place of higher responsibility than he who superintends the education of young men for the sacred office ; for the influence of his instructions, and counsels, and spirit, instead of terminating upon them, diffuses itself all over the Church—but this Seminary has supplied twenty-eight Professors to different Theological Institutions, some of whom, I need not say, have attained to great eminence in their respective departments. What vast im-

portance attaches to our Colleges,—those nurse-
ries of the very flower of the country's intellect;
and how directly is the hand of those who conduct
them upon the springs of our national prosperity—
but of those who have had their training here,
thirty-six have occupied the Presidential chair,
and ninety-four have held Professorships, in these
higher seminaries,—most of them, at the same
time, being, either statedly or occasionally, engaged in preaching the Gospel. Who can measure
the amount of service which they perform for the
Church, who have a primary agency in directing
our great Benevolent Institutions—but twenty-
nine of our alumni have held the Secretaryship of
some or other of these Societies, thus directly
identifying themselves with the progress of the
Gospel at home or abroad. The influence of an
Editor of a widely circulated religious newspaper
or other periodical is exerted so quietly that perhaps the multitude take little note of it; and yet
that same Editor may have a sort of ubiquity in
the Church,—even in the Nation—he may be in
contact with men's minds as a guiding, irresistible
power, where his name has never been heard—he
may sit by his desk, and change the current of
public opinion, or forestall the decisions of eccle-

6

siastical judicatories, without opening his lips; and, when the Sabbath comes, he may be in his own or some other pulpit, proclaiming the Glad Tidings, like any other minister of Christ—but here again, no less than twenty-nine whose names are enrolled on our catalogue, have held this responsible position; and among them are several of our most highly endowed and cultivated minds,—some of whom weekly, and others quarterly, strike chords that vibrate, not now indeed to the extremities of the land, but up to a certain dark, revolting, bloody boundary. And I must not forget to add that the Seminary, especially through its Professors, has contributed largely, in other ways, to our theological and historical literature. If all the books, which have been written on this ground, were gathered, they would not only go far towards forming a library, but among them would be found some of the best productions, in their respective departments, that any language can furnish.

But in all this variety there is perfect *harmony;*— not only no interference, but cordial co-operation. The end aimed at in each of these several departments of active usefulness is the same—all have in view the intellectual and moral renovation of the race, in connection with the progress of a pure

Christianity. It is like some great piece of machinery, each part of which not only performs its own appropriate work, but helps to maintain the harmonious and efficient action of the whole. The Stated Pastor, the Foreign Missionary, the Theological Professor, the President of a College, the Secretary and leading spirit of a great Benevolent Institution, the Editor of a religious newspaper or other periodical,—each has his distinct office, while each becomes, in some sense, an auxiliary to the rest;—sometimes directly,—by supplying the requisite material for others to work upon, or becoming identified with some important effort out of his own immediate range; and sometimes indirectly,—by an example of vigorous application, or perhaps brilliant success.

The influence of this Seminary, I remark again, has been *a conservative, and yet not an unduly restrictive, influence*—it has been adverse to a reckless spirit of innovation, but favourable to healthful progress. The tendency to extremes is one of the qualities that mark the imperfection, not to say perverseness, of our common humanity; but never, perhaps, has this tendency manifested itself so palpably, or in so great a variety of forms, as since this Seminary has been in existence; and hence, to meet the exigency hereby created, we have the new and expressive word, *Ultraism.* It is worthy of remark that this spirit always contemplates, originally, a good object—it always has its basis in truth and right; but, from being exclusively or disproportionately contemplated by an ill-balanced mind, the object either acquires an undue relative importance, or else it suggests the use of unjustifiable means for its accomplishment. I will instance only a single case—that of *Revivals of Religion.* A genuine Revival we all recognize as the richest blessing that God bestows upon his Church; and, in the multiplication of these scenes, we get a foretaste of millennial, even of heavenly, glory. But who needs be told that, in what has been called a Revival, Fanaticism has sometimes performed some of her wildest and most revolting feats; and all the solemnities, even the decencies, of religious worship have been sacrificed; and Satan has counted almost as many self-deceivers as the conductor of the work has counted converts. With this spirit, in none of its various manifestations, has this Seminary ever had any sympathy— its sound, scriptural teachings have been a perpetual rebuke to it; and the impress of sobriety, which its students have received here, has, with comparatively few exceptions, been decisive of their future course. But then, on the other hand, the Seminary has never been alarmed because the world does not stand still—it has never suggested the expediency of stopping short of the point of duty, lest there should be found some temptation there to pass on into the region of extravagance—it has never been slow to admit new thoughts, or to encourage new projects, where they have seemed to originate in wisdom or tend to usefulness. In short, it has sought not to stay the advancing spirit of the age, but to direct it; and sure I am that the verdict of the whole Church is that it has been eminently successful.

It is only an extension, or rather a specific application, of this thought, to say that this Seminary, *while it has been true to the interests of the Presbyterian Church, which it represents, has yet been catholic in its bearing towards other denominations.* That it has always been the faithful supporter and defender of the Presbyterian faith and order, every one, who has been a student here, knows from the character of its teachings; and the whole Church has evidence of it in the general character of those of her ministers who have been educated here; in the manner in which the Seminary has been represented, in her highest judicatory, on questions touching vitally her prosperity; in the fact that the first Professor of Church History and Church Government, while he was yet a Pastor, as well as during the period of his Professorship, published several elaborate and highly popular works, vindicating the claims of Presbyterianism; and, finally, in the many luminous and forcible articles, bearing more or less directly on this subject, which have appeared, from time to time, in the Biblical Repertory. But, while the Seminary has shown itself thoroughly Presbyterian, in character as well as in name, it has never assumed that Presbyterianism is the only divinely accredited form of Christianity—while it has maintained that it is the most perfect embodiment of Scripture truth, in respect to both doctrine and order, it has never set up any exclusive banner; never made its own Shibboleth a term, either of fraternal communion, or of admission to its privileges. Even in the fierce controversy, connected with the second great disruption of the Presbyterian Church, it never placed itself in any needlessly offensive attitude, or counselled to any rash or uncharitable measures; and I venture to say that those of its alumni, who, by that act, were thrown into another body, never lost their filial regard for this their Alma Mater; and that those of them who are with us here to-day, are just as earnest in their devotion, and just as cordial in their congratulations, as if the Assembly of 1837 had confined itself to its ordinary routine of business. But the most decisive testimony on this subject is to be gathered from our General Catalogue; and, if you will glance over it, you will find a large number of names, whose only connection with Presbyterianism is in having a place there. For instance, in the very first class, there was a man who came hither an Episcopalian, and subsequently became a Baptist—the same man has been, and, for aught I know, still is, one of the lights of the Baptist denomination in the South. No less than forty-two, who have been educated here, have found their home, and their field of labour, in the Episcopal Church—and, of these, three have become Bishops;—men, known and honoured by the wise and good of every name; and I doubt not that their large hearts would respond gratefully to our kind remembrances of them. Ninety-two have become ministers in the Congregational Church; fifty-six in the Reformed Dutch Church;

thirty-two in the Baptist Church; eleven in the Associate Reformed and United Presbyterian Church; seven in the German Reformed Church; and five in the Lutheran, and an equal number in the Methodist, Church. A portion of these, indeed, changed their ecclesiastical relations after leaving the Seminary; but many of them did not; and the fact that they could, without embarrassment, pursue their studies here preparatory to the ministry, proves, beyond all question, that they found here an atmosphere, tempered, in a high degree, by the spirit of Christian catholicism. Their distinctive peculiarities they did not indeed hear vindicated—they may have even heard laboured arguments to disprove them; but there has always been a measure of decorum, and dignity, and generous indulgence, pertaining to the spirit of the place, that has made it a happy home even for those whose denominational views are at the greatest remove from those which are here inculcated.

I cannot forbear to say that this Seminary is exerting a *loyal and patriotic, but not an intemperate or indiscriminately condemnatory, influence.* It seems to be the order of Providence that every thing on earth that hath life, whether physical, intellectual, or moral, should have its times for going to sleep. Thus it has been with American Patriotism—the spirit, which worked as fire in the bosoms of our Revolutionary Fathers, had not only lost much of the glow in which it then manifested itself, but had so long been exposed to the wild storms of party, that it seemed threatened with absolute extinction. Wise and thoughtful men were not without fears that Patriotism, in respect to a large part of our population at least, was sinking into her last iron slumber, if she had not actually been arrayed in her death-robes. But the memorable 13th of April, 1861, put to flight that delusion. The balls that struck upon Sumter did a much more potent work than they had bargained for; for, besides achieving an inglorious triumph over a handful of brave but defenceless men, who were on the eve of starvation, they turned the heart of the whole loyal part of the nation into steel. Patriotism had now no longer a dubious existence. Quick as the lightning, she multiplied herself into a host of bright angels, who were going to and fro, delivering lessons upon our perils and duties, and inspiring courage and hope. I do not mean to intimate that this Seminary had ever been indifferent to the interests of the country—

7

she stands too near the spot where WASHINGTON commanded, and MERCER fell,* to be readily suspected of that—but until now there has never been any great occasion to put her to the test: and, since the occasion has come,—thanks to a Gracious Providence,—she does her work nobly;—not by stepping out of her sphere, but by being a unit for the country's unity; especially by sending forth mature thoughts, well considered and weighty arguments, bearing upon the crisis, for the nation to digest and apply. Patriotism, bold, earnest, effective, but yet thoughtful and forbearing, has inscribed her name on the walls, even the very door-posts, of this Seminary; and, in her light, well may the whole country see light and rejoice.

But a painful question here forces itself upon me—How is it that so large a number who have been educated here, with whom many of us have taken sweet counsel, and some of whom we have all delighted to honour,—have identified themselves with an enterprise, designed to lay waste this goodly inheritance which our fathers bequeathed to us? I know many of them so well,

* The memorable battle of Princeton was fought within a few hundred yards of the site of the Seminary.

and they have had a place in my heart so long, that I could not, if I would, answer this question in any other spirit than that of the most enlarged charity. The thought, which I am sure it is most grateful for us to indulge, is, that many of them have just silently bowed to influences which they could not control; and that, when the external pressure comes to be withdrawn, we shall find that, though they have been *in* the Rebellion, they have not been *of* it. And then again, in respect to the large numbers, who, we know, have assumed an attitude of declared hostility to the Government, who needs be told of the blinding influence of circumstances; of the mighty power of hereditary prejudices, of social and domestic relationships, of long established associations, of the eloquence of statesmen, of the general current of example, of the pleas of imagined self-interest, to render both the intellectual and moral vision so confused that good and evil shall seem to have changed places? Who of us can be certain that an influence, which has been so universal, would not have included himself among its victims, if he had come within its range? I am not attempting to make out a justification of our brethren for having fallen into this mad and desolating current;—for that my conscience would not allow me to do—but I submit it to you whether there is not that in their circumstances, which should at least qualify our censure. As for those who have not only been educated here, but have been born and had their home in the North, and are perfectly conversant with Northern manners, and institutions, and influences, and yet have pronounced anathemas upon us in their pulpits,—strengthening the popular delusion that the heart of the whole North never rests from breathing out threatenings and slaughter against the South,—it would be too much to ask for *them* any large measure of indulgence; and yet is it not better to study them as an anomalous specimen of the workings of human nature, than to reciprocate their abuse and crimination? I confess there is not a fact in the whole history of the Church, that confounds me more, than that our Southern brethren should, with such apparent cordiality and unanimity, have lent themselves to this unnatural Rebellion; and yet, I say again, if we obey the dictates of wisdom, we shall forbear all bitter and hostile demonstrations, and shall hold ourselves ready to resume fraternal relations with them, whenever Providence shall open the way for it. Or if that day should never

come, we shall go down to our graves in a brighter
light, and leave a better example to those who
come after us, if, while we have been true to our
country, we have never cast needless reproaches
upon our mistaken brethren.

I only add that this Seminary exerts *a widely
extended and constantly extending influence.* It has
drawn its students, not only from nearly every
State in the Union, but from several European
countries; and from almost every College, from
venerable old Harvard down to those comparatively new lights, which the spirit of Christian
enterprise has kindled up in the Far West. Here,
too, there has been a gathering from all the different classes of society—the sons of the rich and
the great have been here—those who have had
their birth and training in the middle walks of
life, where there is least of temptation and most
of comfort, have been here in crowds—those
whose education has been little else than a con-
stant battle with adverse circumstances, have been
here; and, last of all, the descendants of HAM
have not been without an honourable representation here,—a fact to which we appeal with
confidence as proof that this Seminary has never
endorsed the doctrine that, because, unhappily, a

dark skin has become with us an emblem of servitude, it therefore necessarily involves the curse of ignorance and degradation. Now, between each District, each College, each Class in society, that is thus represented in the Seminary, and the Seminary itself, there is opened, in proportion to the extent of the representation, a channel of reciprocal influence. And then trace the influence which this great body of students, gathered from the four winds, and from such a variety of social positions, exert, as they go forth to their several fields of labour. There is not a city of any extent in the land, where the Gospel has not been sounded forth by some voice or voices that hail from this Seminary. Travel in whatever direction you will, you cannot go far, but that its influence will meet you, either in the form of the living preacher, or in the auspicious results of some ministry upon which the grave has closed. If it were not for the iron gate which the spirit of Rebellion has set up, you might go to the extreme Southern or Southwestern boundary of the country, and find churches not a few, which were supplied, the very last Sabbath, by men whose names appear on our catalogue. If you make your way into the wilderness, the native home of savages, where, half a century ago, the first sign of civilization had not appeared, but where now Christianity holds her well-established dominion, there, again, you will find that this Seminary has had her full share in accomplishing these blessed results. And, finally, if you cross the ocean, and explore the dark domain of Foreign Paganism or Spurious Christianity, you can scarcely pause in any country, and look around you, without finding yourselves in contact with an evangelizing influence that has emanated from Princeton: and if, before you return, you visit the land of our fathers, and put yourselves into communion with the great and good spirits there, you will quickly discover that they are scarcely less familiar with the masterly biblical, theological, historical, and practical works, that our Professors have sent forth, than we are with the choicest of *their* productions. Verily the influence of this Seminary has diffused itself every where, and mingles with every thing! If there is no part of our own country too distant or inaccessible to be reached by it; if it moves upon the great deep of ignorance and superstition in China and India, in France and Italy; if it penetrates into the very darkest part of the heart of Africa; and, finally, if it brings us into close fellowship of thought and feeling with the wise and good all over the world, who will venture, even now, to fix its boundary?

And yet this has been, still is, a *constantly increasing* influence. Some of us remember the time when this great tree, some of whose branches now overshadow other countries, was a mere sapling. We knew then, however, that its seed was good, having been deposited here by the faith and prayers of the Church—we knew that the most skilful hands were employed for its culture, and that the enriching dews of Heavenly grace were not withheld from it; and we had a right to anticipate for it a vigorous and substantial growth; but I doubt not that its history has far more than realized the most sanguine expectations of the most hopeful of its friends. At the time of my own admission to the Seminary, in the fall of 1816, the number of students, if my memory serves me, was about twenty-five; whereas the present number is one hundred and sixty-eight; and I hazard nothing in saying that this numerical increase is a fair index to its general progressive prosperity. I do not say that each successive year has been, in all respects, more proporous than the one immediately preceding; but I do say that, on the whole, it has been constantly growing, not only in numbers, but in resources, in usefulness, in favour with God and man.

And now, in view of the ground we have so rapidly passed over, are we not brought irresistibly to the conclusion that the Princeton Theological Seminary is a mighty power,—well worthy to have attracted us hither on this grateful, commemorative errand? Is there not essentially inherent in it an energy that must necessarily work out grand results? And have not those results already become matter of history, to a sufficient extent to fill us with gratitude for the past, with hope for the future ?

My friends, could we have a more impressive lesson of the vanity of this life of ours, than is found in the fact that, in speaking of this Seminary at the close of the first half century of its existence, we have seemed to be holding converse much more with the dead than with the living? Does not the vast accumulation of stars on our catalogue, diffusing over it an air of funereal gloom, invite us to pause, not more in tender remembrance than solemn reflection? If we glance at the list of our Directors, we find that sixty-three out of a hundred and thirteen have

S

finished their course; and of the twenty, who constituted the original Board in 1812, one venerated name* only remains, unassociated with the grave. On the list of the Board of Trustees, twenty-seven out of fifty-two are starred; and, of the sixteen who composed it in 1825, the name of only one stands without the significant prefix,— and he the solitary survivor of the other Board. Of the ten, who have held Professorships here, only half survive. Of the twenty-four hundred and twenty-two, who have received their theological education here, either partly or wholly, no less than four hundred and eighty-five have gone to give an account of their stewardship. And we, my brethren, are all in the current, which is thus sweeping onward to eternity. When the Centennial Celebration comes round, who of us all, think you, will be here to welcome it? There will be a joyful meeting of kindred spirits then, but they will belong to another generation. May our Gracious Master pour upon us the spirit of wisdom, and strength, and earnest devotion to our

---

* Rev. John McDowell, D. D., whose untiring devotion to the interests of the Seminary, as well as of the Presbyterian Church at large, is already a mattter of history. It was a subject of general regret that he was prevented, by the infirmities of age, from being present to share in the services and enjoyments of the Semi-centennial Jubilee.

high calling, so that, before our places on earth
are vacated, we may build some new monuments
of fidelity in his service, which will at once reflect
fresh honour upon the Institution at which we
have been trained, and encourage and animate
those who shall come after us.

I am quite aware that I have passed the legitimate limit of this exercise, and yet I find other
topics crowding upon my mind, upon which, under
other circumstances, I would gladly speak, and to
which I have no doubt you would heartily and
warmly respond. For instance, I should love to
present to you the Seminary in her relation to
other similar institutions, showing you how nearly
she stands at the head of the list in the order of
time, and tracing her influence in the healthful
growth of some of her younger sisters. I should
love to call your attention to the signs of promise
in respect to the future; to show you that it is
scarcely more certain that the order of Providence
will proceed, than that this Seminary will develope
new powers, and gather increasing glory, in her
onward course. I should love, especially, to try to
re-produce, to those of my own classmates and con-
temporaries in the Seminary who are present,
some of the cherished scenes of those early days;

to remind them of the splendour of LARNED's eloquence; of the charm of NEVINS' wit; of the apostolic simplicity of NEWBOLD; of the thoughtful,
earnest and intensely devout spirit of ARMSTRONG.
But into neither of these fields, attractive as they
are, do I feel at liberty to enter. Nothing remains,
then, but that we leave our united benediction
upon the Seminary, and bid her adieu. We thank
the Directors and Trustees for the wisdom, vigi-
lance, energy, with which they have ordered her
movements, husbanded her resources, and ministered, in various ways, to her efficiency and
strength. We thank the Professors for the ability,
fidelity, constancy, which have ever characterized
their labours, as well as for the cordial welcome with
which they have now greeted us. We congratu-
late the present generation of students on their
advantages, their attainments, their prospects,
and we counsel them to gird themselves with
strength from on high, that they may be prepared to meet the high demands of the age.
We give and record our pledge to the Seminary
that her interests shall be our interests, and
that, when we forget our obligation to her, our
right hand may forget her cunning. We tender
our acknowledgments to the inhabitants of this

ancient and honoured town for the cordial and graceful hospitality which we have found in their dwellings, and in which some of us recognize only a re-production of what we used to witness in their fathers and mothers, who have fallen asleep. We ratify afresh our vows of fraternal fellowship with each other, thanking God for this happy meeting, and sending our thoughts and hopes forward to a glorious renewal of our intercourse, where the meeting shall be, not for a day, but for eternity. The hallowed scenes through which we are now passing shall never fade from our memories,—no, never. We will dwell upon them—we will cherish them—we will embalm them—they shall make all our thoughts of this beloved spot more precious; and we will gather from them a fresh stimulus to the prosecution of our onward, upward journey.

APPENDIX.*

The Celebration of the Fiftieth Anniversary of the establishment of the Theological Seminary of the Presbyterian Church in Princeton, took place on the 30th of April, 1862, agreeably to a plan, of which notice had been extensively given. The day was one of the most beautiful and balmy of the whole year. Many hundreds of the Alumni of the Seminary were present, and with them many brethren of other denominations, who joined heartily in all the exercises of the occasion. There were many clergymen from the Congregational, the Episcopal, the Reformed Dutch, the Baptist Churches, and the several families of Presbyterians, who seemed as much at home on that delightful spot and in that goodly company, as if they had not only been born and nurtured, but always dwelt, in the same ecclesiastical household.

The Alumni met at eleven o'clock in the First Presbyterian Church. The Rev. Dr. MAGIE, of Elizabeth, N. J., was chosen to preside, and the Rev. Dr. PAXTON, of the Allegheny Theological Seminary, was appointed Secretary. Dr. Magie, on taking the chair, made a few pertinent remarks, expressive of the great pleasure it afforded him to mingle in the exercises of the day, and of his deep sense of obligation to the Seminary, which he should carry with him to his grave.

The Rev. Dr. YEOMANS, being called upon, led in prayer.

* This account of the proceedings of the day is taken, substantially, from the New York Observer.

The Committee, who had arranged the meeting, stated that no order of exercises had been agreed upon, but that they had prepared a Report, leaving it to those who should speak on the Resolutions to select their own topics. The following is the Report submitted, and subsequently adopted :—

1. The Alumni of the Princeton Theological Seminary, assembled to celebrate its Fiftieth Anniversary, record with devout gratitude their sense of the great goodness of God to this Institution. We especially recognize his beneficent Providence in raising up those two venerated men, ARCHIBALD ALEXANDER and SAMUEL MILLER, to become its first Professors, and in sparing them to conduct its affairs with pre-eminent wisdom and fidelity for forty years.

2. In the General Catalogue of the Seminary just issued, we find the following summary of its History :—

Whole number of Students	2422
Dead	485
Connected with the Seminary the present year	168
Foreign Missionaries	127
Appointed Foreign Missionaries	7
Professors in Theological Seminaries	28
Presidents of Colleges	36
Professors in Colleges	94
Directors of this Seminary	17
Moderators of the General Assembly	8

We refrain from any attempt to gather up the weighty results which a half century must have accumulated in the train of an army of faithful labourers like this. A glance at the table will show that the healthful influences, emanating from this source, have radiated far and wide in every direction; that, apart from the spiritual benefits conferred on some thousands of churches, this Seminary has had an important agency in moulding our systems of popular education, and in training the public men of the country, and that many a Pagan land has reason to bless God that it has been established. We rejoice in all the good which has been effected through these various channels; and we re-assure our brethren, especially those in Heathen countries, that they are not forgotten as we gather around our *Alma Mater* to-day.

3. It is a matter of sincere gratitude with us, that our Seminary has never faltered in its maintenance of the ancient faith of the Apostolic Church, and that, through the writings of its Professors and Alumni, it has made large and valuable contributions to Biblical Criticism and Theological Science; achieving for itself a reputation in these departments which has commanded the respect of the best scholars of Europe and of our own country.

4. In view of the distrust so often expressed respecting Theological Seminaries, we deem it proper to re-affirm our hearty approval of the principles embodied in the plan of this Institution and illustrated in its history : the system adopted here commends itself to us, at the close of a half century, as eminently wise, scriptural and efficient : and the Seminary was never more worthy of the confidence of the Church than it is at this moment. In accounting for this result, we may refer not only, under Providence, to the eminent learning and ability of the Professors who have filled its various chairs, but to the spirit of genuine piety which has uniformly pervaded and controlled its entire administration. While keeping well abreast with the age in the general progress of Biblical science and polite literature, it has been the paramount law of this School of the Prophets to subordinate the intellectual to the spiritual, and never to exalt speculative theology at the expense of personal religious experience. This is the true glory of our Seminary, and herein, under God, lies the secret of its power and success.

5. In the pervading spirit of our venerable Seminary we recognize that true catholicity of feeling, combined with an inflexible adherence to sound doctrine, by which our Church has always been distinguished. And in this characteristic we find an explanation of the grateful fact, that our sister churches are so often represented on its catalogues; as they

9

have also sent some of their most honoured sons to take part in this commemoration.

6. We record with reverence and submission the ravages which death has made among the Directors, the Faculty, and the Alumni of our Seminary. May we pay the best of all tributes to their memory, by following them in so far as they followed Christ.

7. We offer our united and hearty thanks to the numerous benefactors of our beloved Seminary. We respectfully remind the Church it has so long adorned and blessed, that its funds are still very inadequate to its needs. And we propose to our fellow-alumni, whenever the dark cloud which now overshadows the land shall have passed away, that a united effort be made to complete its endowment, and establish its financial interests upon a broad and generous foundation.

All the exercises of the morning, with the exception of the above resolutions, though highly felicitous, were evidently unpremeditated; and, as no provision was made to secure the speeches at the time of their delivery, all that can be done is to barely hint at them. Dr. HODGE was called upon to speak, as having been the associate of Dr. MILLER and Dr. ALEXANDER; and, though he responded reluctantly, from being impressed with the idea that it was unsuitable that his voice should be heard on the occasion, his remarks were characterized by great appropriateness, and by a pathos that was quite irresistible. He remarked that when the two venerable men, who had been named, were made Professors, he was but a mere youth, and that when he was elected to be associated with them, he felt like sitting on a stool at their feet. Dr. Alexander took him by the hand as if he were a child, and in that relation he had always loved to regard himself; and for him to speak on this occasion was like making remarks at the funeral of one's own father. He paid a touching tribute to the memory of both these admirable men. He had seen them under various forms of trial, but had never heard a word from either which the purest angel would have stopped on their lips, nor any manifestation of feeling toward each other, which God Himself would not approve. It was a pleasure to him to bear such a testimony concerning these holy men in the presence of such an audience, before he died. The Seminary had now a history, world-wide, that could not be altered—and who had given it such a history? Dr. Alexander and Dr. Miller, whose shoes' latchet he was not worthy to unloose.

The Rev. Dr. CHARLES BEATTY, of Steubenville, O., said he was one of the earliest of the alumni, and reared almost in sight of the Seminary ; and, when he was licensed to preach, Dr. Alexander came to him, and, taking him by the hand, said " God bless you, my son ;" "and I feel that grasp," said he, " as though it had been but yesterday."

The Rev. Dr. HOWARD MALCOM, of the Baptist Church, said there were two features in the character of the Seminary and its Professors, to which he wished to bear testimony ; and his testimony was as follows :— " It is an eminently catholic institution. I am a Baptist. I came hither a Baptist, and went away a Baptist. I never heard any thing here that injured my feelings. The subject of Infant Baptism was discussed, but never in an unkind spirit. I have two sons who are Baptists, and both of them were educated here. 2d. I have never known an institution where personal piety was more studiously cultivated. The whole surrounding atmosphere seemed impregnated with the spirit of devotion."

The Rev. Dr. Chickering, of Portland, Me., being called upon as a minister of another denomination, (Congregational), said that some who had preceded him apologized for not having expected to speak, " but if any have come thus," said he, " I more "—and besides he had come almost out of breath, for he had travelled three hundred and fifty miles in twenty-four hours, stopping four hours in Boston, and one in Jersey City. He counted it a joy to be there. He had not come as a denominational representative. New England had heard of Dr. Miller and Dr. Alexander, and he had found himself so much at home that he had quite forgotten that he was not an alumnus, and had detected himself in voting on the Resolutions. "And," said he, " I like the name of your great annual assemblage,— the General Assembly—it is both scriptural and impressive."

The Rev. Dr. Plumer repeated the names of many of the early alumni, who, with the venerated Professors, had gone to the Heavenly mansions; among whom were the beloved Nevins, and Douglass, and Graham—but it was not of those of whom he wished then to speak—it was of his *Elder Brother*, the Lord Jesus Christ—to Him belonged the glory of all the influence and success of the Institution. It was on his head that he wished to place the crown.

Interesting and impressive remarks were made by Professor Fisher, of Yale College, who paid a beautiful tribute to the memory of Dr. James W. Alexander; by the Rev. Dr. Baird, who related a conversation that he had with Dr. Chalmers, in which the great Scotch divine spoke in most glowing terms of both Dr. Alexander and Dr. Miller; and by some others.

The following interesting letter was received from the Rev. Dr. Swift, of Allegheny City:—

ALLEGHENY, April 18, 1862.

The contemplated meeting of the Alumni of the Theological Seminary at Princeton:

HONOURED AND DEAR BRETHREN: I feel it a privation to be unable to mingle my fraternal congratulations with yours, and share with you in the sacred and congenial pleasures of this fiftieth anniversary of our venerated Seminary. Surely you will find it intellectually and spiritually "good to be there," and may our blessed Lord be with you and refresh your hearts. When I recur to the fact that I became a member of the Seminary in 1814, about eighteen months after its opening, and when Dr. Miller had just arrived to assume the duties of his office, and our entire roll of students numbered but little over twenty, I am reminded solemnly that, if I were present with you to-day, I should find few of my cotemporaries to greet. If I asked for Blain, and Blatchford, and Huntington, and McDowell, and Stanton, and Wood, and Cruikshanks, and Edgar, and Green, and Searle, and Smith, and Talmage, and Wilbur and Chamberlain, and Crow, and Gilbert, and Henry, and Mills, and Judd, and Larned, and others, this side the grave and of Heaven, I should ask in vain. The dwelling I might perhaps find, where our class, for a time, met for recitation in Dr. Miller's parlor, and the other humble dwelling where Dr. Alexander lived, and where one of our number instructed his sons, *James* and *Addison*, then but sprightly lads. Without an edifice and without a library, we borrowed our common recitation room and our books from the College of New Jersey: and the life of our infant Seminary was a life of faith and of hope, having indeed a pledge of a continued and growing life in the possession of two of the ablest and best instructors which Protestant Christendom then contained.

It was on a spring morning, during the period of our residence in the Seminary, that the village population beheld the novel yet noble spectacle of our little band, without pomp or music, emerging from the College Campus, and marching out, headed by Drs. Green, Alexander and Miller, and a few Directors, to an adjacent field, where, with devout supplication, the first named was to lay the corner-stone of the Seminary edifice.

In the comparative destitution of funds to erect this single building ; in the fewness of the spectators and the simplicity of our little, feeble host of students, there was, in that scene, to the eye of mere worldly aspiration, perhaps an almost ridiculous absurdity in the act of beginning to build with such a prospect. But when these venerable men uncovered their heads, and the words of faith, and prayer, and consecration of all to Christ, broke upon the air of that calm and tranquil morning ; when it was asked, in tones of mellowed and holy earnestness, that this intended edifice (itself as yet but the object of faith) might be reared up as a lasting monument of God's goodness to the Presbyterian Church, and that, for Christ's glory, it might be the educational home of many generations of his ministers who should carry the everlasting gospel to all nations, there was in those utterances of humble confidence in Christ, and lofty expansive expectation, a sublimity and power which every heart must have felt. That morning the Mediator of the new covenant was there, and ever since He has been fulfilling the petitions of that hour. The years which we have since seen, have, many of them, been years of disaster and trial to our Zion; and large portions of it, then represented there, have been sundered from its pale; and these noble devoted fathers, and almost all the brethren then present, have passed away; but the venerable Seminary has moved on with unfaltering prosperity, and expanding usefulness : and it is a source of gratitude to God that, for these fifty years, no one of her Professors has, either by defection in doctrine or inconsistency of practice, brought the slightest stain upon her honoured name. Her pupils, also, have, to a remarkable extent, been free from cases of apostacy, and have faithfully served the Church at home and in distant lands.

Some fifteen or twenty years ago, in a casual conversation, the present senior Professor, with his characteristic humility and self-distrust, said to me, "When these well-known and eminent Fathers shall be gone, Princeton, away from the geographical centre of the Church, will no longer have the attractions and the central influence which she once had." I did not tell him what I thought of this. I did not tell him that I had been present on that morning when its corner stone was laid, and felt assured that, as to Princeton, her onward career was then written in Heaven.

In the progress of events, I have been called to co-operate in founding and sustaining another Seminary of our Church; and have, with my brethren, rejoiced and given thanks to Christ for its success hitherto; but I have, in doing this, lost nothing of my earliest love to Princeton. My faith would not permit me to think, nor my heart permit me to desire, that any thing should impair the influence, or impede the growth, of this our first and model Institution. Much we may, my beloved Brethren, yet do for it, in our various spheres of duty, and we who are old, by our fervent prayers.

The close of another fifty years none of us will be here to witness; but if we are faithful, what a glorious epoch may it be amidst the long hallowed scenes of Princeton! How many distant lands will have pronounced its name! How many additional venerated dead will have bound the sacred memories of the Church to the cemetery which slumbers at its side!

Beloved Brethren, may our Gracious Lord bless your happy and sacred convocation with his especial presence, and make your communion sweet. May your rejoicings for what He has already done for Princeton be as the gladness of a morning, whose light shall shine more and more unto the perfect day.

With Christian love and fraternal salutations,

Yours, truly,

E. P. SWIFT.

At the close of the meeting, the Alumni of the Seminary, together with all the strangers present, were invited to the Seminary grounds, where a bountiful and even splendid dinner had been provided, of which several hundred partook, the occasion being one of rare social enjoyment. An hour or more was here spent in reviving old associations, the ladies, in the mean time, having been invited to the houses of the Professors and other citizens, which had been thrown open to all who were disposed to share their hospitalities.

The interesting scene at the Seminary grounds was very agreeably varied by an announcement, coming from the Board of Trustees, that Messrs. ROBERT L. and ALEXANDER STUART, of New York, had just contributed fifty thousand dollars to the funds of the Seminary, in honour of its Fiftieth Anniversary. It was received with shouts of applause, and added not a little to the enjoyment of the occasion.

At three o'clock in the afternoon, the Alumni, according to previous arrangement, re-assembled in the church, and with them a large number of the inhabitants of the town, and of strangers from various parts of the country,—filling the edifice to its utmost capacity. The Commemorative Discourse was preceded by a prayer from the Rev. Dr. JACOBUS, Professor in the Allegheny Theological Seminary, and followed by another, from the Rev. Dr. POTTS, of New York; after which, the Rev. Dr. BACKUS, of Baltimore, offered a resolution for the printing of the Discourse which had been delivered, which was unanimously adopted. The exercises were concluded by the singing of the Doxology, by the immense congregation, and the pronouncing of the Benediction, by Dr. Potts. The multitude of brethren then dispersed, with their hearts filled with gratitude and gladness by the hallowed exercises of the day.